50 Warmer Soup Recipes for Home

By: Kelly Johnson

Table of Contents

- Classic Chicken Noodle Soup
- Creamy Tomato Basil Soup
- Spicy Lentil Soup
- Minestrone Soup
- Potato Leek Soup
- Butternut Squash Soup
- French Onion Soup
- Beef and Barley Soup
- Chicken Tortilla Soup
- Thai Coconut Curry Soup
- Split Pea Soup
- Cream of Mushroom Soup
- Mexican Black Bean Soup
- Roasted Red Pepper Soup
- Vegetable Curry Soup
- Italian Wedding Soup
- Clam Chowder
- Chicken and Rice Soup
- Sweet Potato and Kale Soup
- Moroccan Chickpea Soup
- Lemon Chicken Orzo Soup
- Creamy Cauliflower Soup
- Shrimp and Corn Chowder
- Spinach and White Bean Soup
- Turkey Chili
- Broccoli Cheddar Soup
- Sausage and Kale Soup
- Zucchini and Corn Chowder
- Carrot Ginger Soup
- Quinoa and Vegetable Soup
- Creamy Chicken and Wild Rice Soup
- Black-eyed Pea Soup
- Cabbage Roll Soup
- Hungarian Goulash Soup
- Mediterranean Fish Soup

- Pumpkin Curry Soup
- Lemon Dill Chicken Soup
- Thai Tom Yum Soup
- Corn and Potato Chowder
- Chicken and Dumpling Soup
- Soba Noodle Soup
- Cuban Black Bean Soup
- Irish Potato Soup
- Chicken Gumbo
- White Bean and Escarole Soup
- Tofu Miso Soup
- Tomato and Quinoa Soup
- Sweet Corn and Bacon Chowder
- Italian Sausage and Kale Soup
- Avocado Lime Chicken Soup

Classic Chicken Noodle Soup

Ingredients:

- 1 tablespoon olive oil
- 1 onion, diced
- 3 carrots, sliced
- 3 celery stalks, sliced
- 3 cloves garlic, minced
- 8 cups chicken broth
- 1 bay leaf
- 1 teaspoon dried thyme
- 1 teaspoon dried oregano
- 2 cups shredded cooked chicken
- 2 cups egg noodles
- Salt and pepper to taste
- Fresh parsley for garnish

Instructions:

In a large pot, heat the olive oil over medium heat. Add the diced onion, sliced carrots, and sliced celery. Cook until the vegetables are softened, about 5-7 minutes.
Add the minced garlic and cook for an additional 1-2 minutes until fragrant.
Pour in the chicken broth, and add the bay leaf, dried thyme, and dried oregano. Bring the mixture to a simmer.
Add the shredded cooked chicken to the pot. Simmer for 10-15 minutes until the chicken is heated through and the flavors meld.
In the last 5 minutes of cooking, add the egg noodles to the pot. Cook until the noodles are tender.
Season the soup with salt and pepper to taste. Remove the bay leaf.
Ladle the soup into bowls, and garnish with fresh parsley.
Serve hot and enjoy your classic chicken noodle soup!

Creamy Tomato Basil Soup

Ingredients:

- 2 tablespoons olive oil
- 1 onion, chopped
- 3 cloves garlic, minced
- 2 cans (28 ounces each) whole tomatoes, undrained
- 1 can (14 ounces) diced tomatoes, undrained
- 2 cups vegetable or chicken broth
- 1 teaspoon sugar
- 1 teaspoon dried basil
- 1/2 teaspoon dried oregano
- 1/2 teaspoon salt
- 1/4 teaspoon black pepper
- 1 cup heavy cream
- Fresh basil leaves for garnish (optional)

Instructions:

In a large pot, heat the olive oil over medium heat. Add the chopped onion and cook until softened, about 5 minutes.
Add the minced garlic and cook for an additional 1-2 minutes until fragrant.
Pour in the whole tomatoes and diced tomatoes with their juices. Break up the whole tomatoes with a spoon or spatula.
Add the vegetable or chicken broth, sugar, dried basil, dried oregano, salt, and black pepper. Stir to combine.
Bring the soup to a simmer and let it cook for 15-20 minutes to allow the flavors to meld.
Using an immersion blender, blend the soup until smooth. If you don't have an immersion blender, carefully transfer the soup in batches to a blender and blend until smooth. Be cautious with hot liquids.
Return the blended soup to the pot, and stir in the heavy cream. Cook for an additional 5 minutes, stirring occasionally.
Taste and adjust the seasoning if necessary.
Ladle the creamy tomato basil soup into bowls, and garnish with fresh basil leaves if desired. Serve hot and enjoy this comforting and creamy tomato basil soup!

Spicy Lentil Soup

Ingredients:

- 2 tablespoons olive oil
- 1 onion, finely chopped
- 3 carrots, diced
- 3 celery stalks, diced
- 3 cloves garlic, minced
- 1 cup dried green or brown lentils, rinsed and drained
- 1 can (14 ounces) diced tomatoes
- 6 cups vegetable or chicken broth
- 1 teaspoon ground cumin
- 1/2 teaspoon ground coriander
- 1/2 teaspoon smoked paprika
- 1/4 teaspoon cayenne pepper (adjust to taste for spice level)
- Salt and black pepper to taste
- Juice of 1 lemon
- Fresh cilantro for garnish (optional)
- Greek yogurt or sour cream for serving (optional)

Instructions:

In a large pot, heat the olive oil over medium heat. Add the chopped onion, diced carrots, and diced celery. Cook until the vegetables are softened, about 5-7 minutes.
Add the minced garlic and cook for an additional 1-2 minutes until fragrant.
Stir in the rinsed lentils, diced tomatoes (with their juices), and vegetable or chicken broth.
Add ground cumin, ground coriander, smoked paprika, cayenne pepper, salt, and black pepper. Stir to combine.
Bring the soup to a boil, then reduce the heat to low, cover, and simmer for 25-30 minutes or until the lentils are tender.
Squeeze in the juice of 1 lemon and stir to combine.
Taste the soup and adjust the seasoning if needed.
Ladle the spicy lentil soup into bowls, and garnish with fresh cilantro if desired.
Serve hot with a dollop of Greek yogurt or sour cream if you like.
Enjoy this flavorful and spicy lentil soup as a comforting meal!

Minestrone Soup

Ingredients:

- 2 tablespoons olive oil
- 1 onion, finely chopped
- 3 cloves garlic, minced
- 2 carrots, diced
- 2 celery stalks, diced
- 1 zucchini, diced
- 1 cup green beans, cut into bite-sized pieces
- 1 can (14 ounces) diced tomatoes
- 1 can (14 ounces) kidney beans, drained and rinsed
- 1 can (14 ounces) cannellini beans, drained and rinsed
- 6 cups vegetable broth
- 1 teaspoon dried oregano
- 1 teaspoon dried basil
- 1/2 teaspoon dried thyme
- 1/2 cup small pasta (such as ditalini or elbow macaroni)
- Salt and black pepper to taste
- 2 cups fresh spinach or kale, chopped
- Grated Parmesan cheese for serving (optional)

Instructions:

In a large pot, heat the olive oil over medium heat. Add the chopped onion and cook until softened, about 5 minutes.
Add the minced garlic and cook for an additional 1-2 minutes until fragrant.
Add the diced carrots, diced celery, diced zucchini, and green beans to the pot. Cook for 5-7 minutes until the vegetables start to soften.
Pour in the diced tomatoes, kidney beans, cannellini beans, and vegetable broth. Add dried oregano, dried basil, dried thyme, and bring the soup to a boil.
Stir in the pasta and cook according to the package instructions or until al dente.
Season the soup with salt and black pepper to taste.
In the last 5 minutes of cooking, add the chopped spinach or kale. Cook until the greens are wilted.
Taste and adjust the seasoning if needed.
Ladle the minestrone soup into bowls, and top with grated Parmesan cheese if desired.

Serve hot and enjoy this hearty and nutritious minestrone soup!

Potato Leek Soup

Ingredients:

- 3 tablespoons unsalted butter
- 3 leeks, white and light green parts, thinly sliced
- 3 cloves garlic, minced
- 4 large potatoes, peeled and diced
- 6 cups vegetable or chicken broth
- 1 bay leaf
- 1 teaspoon dried thyme
- Salt and black pepper to taste
- 1 cup whole milk or heavy cream
- Chives or fresh parsley for garnish (optional)

Instructions:

In a large pot, melt the butter over medium heat. Add the sliced leeks and cook until softened, about 5 minutes.
Add the minced garlic and cook for an additional 1-2 minutes until fragrant.
Add the diced potatoes, vegetable or chicken broth, bay leaf, dried thyme, salt, and black pepper. Stir to combine.
Bring the soup to a boil, then reduce the heat to low, cover, and simmer for 20-25 minutes or until the potatoes are tender.
Remove the bay leaf from the pot.
Use an immersion blender to blend the soup until smooth. Alternatively, carefully transfer the soup in batches to a blender and blend until smooth. Be cautious with hot liquids.
Return the blended soup to the pot, and stir in the whole milk or heavy cream.
Taste and adjust the seasoning if needed.
Simmer the soup for an additional 5 minutes to heat through.
Ladle the potato leek soup into bowls, and garnish with chives or fresh parsley if desired.
Serve hot and enjoy the creamy and comforting potato leek soup!

Butternut Squash Soup

Ingredients:

- 1 large butternut squash, peeled, seeded, and diced
- 2 tablespoons olive oil
- 1 onion, chopped
- 3 carrots, peeled and chopped
- 3 cloves garlic, minced
- 1 apple, peeled, cored, and chopped
- 4 cups vegetable or chicken broth
- 1 teaspoon ground cinnamon
- 1/2 teaspoon ground nutmeg
- 1/2 teaspoon ground ginger
- Salt and black pepper to taste
- 1 cup coconut milk or heavy cream
- Toasted pumpkin seeds for garnish (optional)
- Fresh thyme or parsley for garnish (optional)

Instructions:

Preheat the oven to 400°F (200°C).
Place the diced butternut squash on a baking sheet. Drizzle with olive oil, season with salt and pepper, and toss to coat. Roast in the preheated oven for about 25-30 minutes or until the squash is tender and lightly browned.
In a large pot, heat olive oil over medium heat. Add the chopped onion and carrots, and cook until softened, about 5-7 minutes.
Add the minced garlic and chopped apple to the pot. Cook for an additional 3-4 minutes until fragrant.
Add the roasted butternut squash to the pot, along with the vegetable or chicken broth, ground cinnamon, ground nutmeg, and ground ginger. Stir to combine.
Bring the soup to a simmer and let it cook for 15-20 minutes to allow the flavors to meld.
Use an immersion blender to blend the soup until smooth. Alternatively, transfer the soup in batches to a blender and blend until smooth. Be cautious with hot liquids.
Stir in the coconut milk or heavy cream and season with additional salt and black pepper if needed.
Simmer the soup for an additional 5 minutes to heat through.

Ladle the butternut squash soup into bowls, and garnish with toasted pumpkin seeds and fresh thyme or parsley if desired.
Serve hot and enjoy this velvety and flavorful butternut squash soup!

French Onion Soup

Ingredients:

- 4 large onions, thinly sliced
- 3 tablespoons unsalted butter
- 2 tablespoons olive oil
- 2 cloves garlic, minced
- 1 teaspoon sugar
- 1/2 cup dry white wine (optional)
- 4 cups beef broth
- 2 cups chicken broth
- 1 bay leaf
- 1 teaspoon dried thyme
- Salt and black pepper to taste
- Baguette, sliced
- Gruyère or Swiss cheese, grated
- Fresh parsley for garnish (optional)

Instructions:

In a large pot, melt the butter and olive oil over medium heat. Add the thinly sliced onions and cook, stirring occasionally, until the onions are caramelized and golden brown, about 25-30 minutes.

Add minced garlic and sugar to the caramelized onions. Cook for an additional 2-3 minutes until the garlic is fragrant.

If using white wine, pour it into the pot to deglaze, scraping any browned bits from the bottom. Allow the wine to cook down for a few minutes.

Add beef broth, chicken broth, bay leaf, dried thyme, salt, and black pepper to the pot. Bring the soup to a simmer and let it cook for an additional 15-20 minutes to allow the flavors to meld.

While the soup is simmering, preheat the broiler in your oven.

Place slices of baguette on a baking sheet and toast them under the broiler until they are golden brown on both sides.

Remove the bay leaf from the soup and adjust the seasoning if needed.

Ladle the French onion soup into oven-safe bowls. Place a slice or two of toasted baguette on top of each bowl.

Sprinkle a generous amount of grated Gruyère or Swiss cheese over the bread slices.

Place the bowls under the broiler until the cheese is melted and bubbly, about 2-3 minutes.
Garnish with fresh parsley if desired.
Carefully remove the bowls from the oven, as they will be hot.
Serve hot and enjoy this classic French Onion Soup with gooey, melted cheese on top!

Beef and Barley Soup

Ingredients:

- 1 pound (450g) beef stew meat, cut into bite-sized pieces
- 2 tablespoons olive oil
- 1 onion, finely chopped
- 3 carrots, diced
- 3 celery stalks, diced
- 3 cloves garlic, minced
- 1 cup pearl barley, rinsed and drained
- 8 cups beef broth
- 1 can (14 ounces) diced tomatoes
- 2 bay leaves
- 1 teaspoon dried thyme
- Salt and black pepper to taste
- Fresh parsley for garnish (optional)

Instructions:

In a large pot, heat the olive oil over medium heat. Add the beef stew meat and brown on all sides. Remove the beef from the pot and set aside.
In the same pot, add chopped onion, diced carrots, and diced celery. Cook until the vegetables are softened, about 5 minutes.
Add minced garlic and cook for an additional 1-2 minutes until fragrant.
Return the browned beef to the pot and add rinsed barley, beef broth, diced tomatoes (with their juices), bay leaves, dried thyme, salt, and black pepper. Stir to combine.
Bring the soup to a boil, then reduce the heat to low, cover, and simmer for 45-60 minutes or until the beef is tender and the barley is cooked.
Remove the bay leaves from the pot and discard.
Taste the soup and adjust the seasoning if necessary.
Ladle the beef and barley soup into bowls, and garnish with fresh parsley if desired.
Serve hot and enjoy this hearty and flavorful beef and barley soup!

Chicken Tortilla Soup

Ingredients:

- 1 tablespoon vegetable oil
- 1 onion, finely chopped
- 3 cloves garlic, minced
- 1 jalapeño, seeded and minced (optional for heat)
- 1 teaspoon ground cumin
- 1 teaspoon chili powder
- 1 can (14 ounces) diced tomatoes
- 1 can (4 ounces) diced green chilies
- 6 cups chicken broth
- 1 pound (450g) boneless, skinless chicken breasts, cooked and shredded
- 1 cup corn kernels (fresh or frozen)
- 1 cup black beans, drained and rinsed
- Salt and black pepper to taste
- Juice of 1 lime
- Fresh cilantro for garnish
- Tortilla strips or tortilla chips for serving
- Avocado slices for garnish (optional)
- Shredded cheese for garnish (optional)
- Sour cream for garnish (optional)

Instructions:

In a large pot, heat the vegetable oil over medium heat. Add the chopped onion and cook until softened, about 5 minutes.
Add minced garlic and jalapeño (if using) to the pot. Cook for an additional 1-2 minutes until fragrant.
Stir in ground cumin and chili powder, and cook for another minute.
Add diced tomatoes, diced green chilies, and chicken broth to the pot. Bring the soup to a simmer.
Add shredded chicken, corn kernels, and black beans to the pot. Season with salt and black pepper to taste. Simmer for 15-20 minutes to allow the flavors to meld.
Stir in the lime juice just before serving.
Taste the soup and adjust the seasoning if necessary.
Ladle the chicken tortilla soup into bowls, and garnish with fresh cilantro.

Serve hot, and top with tortilla strips or chips, avocado slices, shredded cheese, and a dollop of sour cream if desired.
Enjoy this delicious and comforting chicken tortilla soup!

Thai Coconut Curry Soup

Ingredients:

- 1 tablespoon vegetable oil
- 1 onion, finely chopped
- 3 cloves garlic, minced
- 1 tablespoon ginger, grated
- 2 tablespoons red curry paste
- 4 cups vegetable or chicken broth
- 1 can (14 ounces) coconut milk
- 1 pound (450g) chicken breast, thinly sliced (optional)
- 1 red bell pepper, thinly sliced
- 1 carrot, julienned
- 1 zucchini, julienned
- 1 cup mushrooms, sliced
- 2 tablespoons soy sauce
- 1 tablespoon fish sauce (optional)
- 1 tablespoon brown sugar
- Juice of 1 lime
- Salt and pepper to taste
- Fresh cilantro for garnish
- Red pepper flakes for extra heat (optional)
- Cooked rice or rice noodles for serving

Instructions:

In a large pot, heat the vegetable oil over medium heat. Add the chopped onion and cook until softened, about 5 minutes.
Add minced garlic and grated ginger to the pot. Cook for an additional 1-2 minutes until fragrant.
Stir in the red curry paste and cook for another minute.
Pour in the vegetable or chicken broth and coconut milk. Bring the soup to a simmer.
If using chicken, add the thinly sliced chicken to the pot and let it cook until no longer pink.
Add sliced red bell pepper, julienned carrot, julienned zucchini, and sliced mushrooms to the pot. Simmer for 5-7 minutes until the vegetables are tender.

Stir in soy sauce, fish sauce (if using), brown sugar, and lime juice. Season with salt and pepper to taste.
Taste the soup and adjust the seasoning if necessary.
Ladle the Thai coconut curry soup over cooked rice or rice noodles in bowls.
Garnish with fresh cilantro and red pepper flakes if you like.
Serve hot and enjoy this flavorful and aromatic Thai coconut curry soup!

Split Pea Soup

Ingredients:

- 1 tablespoon olive oil
- 1 onion, chopped
- 2 carrots, diced
- 2 celery stalks, diced
- 3 cloves garlic, minced
- 2 cups dried green split peas, rinsed and drained
- 8 cups vegetable or ham broth
- 1 bay leaf
- 1 teaspoon dried thyme
- 1/2 teaspoon dried oregano
- Salt and black pepper to taste
- 1 ham hock or 1 cup diced ham (optional)
- 1 cup potatoes, diced (optional)
- 1 cup leeks, sliced (optional)
- Fresh parsley for garnish (optional)

Instructions:

In a large pot, heat the olive oil over medium heat. Add the chopped onion, diced carrots, and diced celery. Cook until the vegetables are softened, about 5-7 minutes.
Add minced garlic and cook for an additional 1-2 minutes until fragrant.
Add the rinsed split peas, vegetable or ham broth, bay leaf, dried thyme, dried oregano, salt, and black pepper to the pot. If using, add the ham hock for added flavor.
If using additional ingredients like diced ham, potatoes, or leeks, add them to the pot.
Bring the soup to a boil, then reduce the heat to low, cover, and simmer for 1 to 1.5 hours or until the split peas are tender.
If using a ham hock, remove it from the pot and shred the meat, then return it to the soup.
Taste the soup and adjust the seasoning if needed.
Remove the bay leaf from the pot.
Ladle the split pea soup into bowls, and garnish with fresh parsley if desired.

Serve hot and enjoy this comforting and hearty split pea soup!

Cream of Mushroom Soup

Ingredients:

- 2 tablespoons unsalted butter
- 1 onion, chopped
- 2 cloves garlic, minced
- 1 pound (450g) mushrooms, sliced
- 1/4 cup all-purpose flour
- 4 cups vegetable or chicken broth
- 1 cup milk or heavy cream
- 1 teaspoon dried thyme
- Salt and black pepper to taste
- 2 tablespoons dry white wine (optional)
- Chopped fresh parsley for garnish (optional)

Instructions:

In a large pot, melt the butter over medium heat. Add the chopped onion and cook until softened, about 5 minutes.
Add minced garlic and sliced mushrooms to the pot. Cook for 8-10 minutes until the mushrooms release their moisture and become golden brown.
Sprinkle flour over the mushrooms and stir to combine. Cook for 2-3 minutes to eliminate the raw flour taste.
Gradually whisk in the vegetable or chicken broth, making sure there are no lumps. Bring the mixture to a simmer.
Stir in the milk or heavy cream, dried thyme, salt, and black pepper. If using, add the dry white wine.
Simmer the soup for 15-20 minutes, stirring occasionally, until it thickens and the flavors meld.
Taste the soup and adjust the seasoning if necessary.
Remove the pot from heat and use an immersion blender to puree the soup until smooth. Alternatively, carefully transfer the soup in batches to a blender and blend until smooth. Be cautious with hot liquids.
Return the blended soup to the pot and heat through.
Ladle the cream of mushroom soup into bowls, and garnish with chopped fresh parsley if desired.
Serve hot and enjoy this velvety and rich cream of mushroom soup!

Mexican Black Bean Soup

Ingredients:

- 2 tablespoons olive oil
- 1 onion, chopped
- 2 cloves garlic, minced
- 1 red bell pepper, chopped
- 1 jalapeño, seeded and minced
- 2 teaspoons ground cumin
- 1 teaspoon chili powder
- 1 teaspoon smoked paprika
- 2 cans (15 ounces each) black beans, drained and rinsed
- 1 can (14 ounces) diced tomatoes
- 4 cups vegetable or chicken broth
- 1 cup corn kernels (fresh or frozen)
- Salt and black pepper to taste
- Juice of 1 lime
- Fresh cilantro for garnish
- Avocado slices for garnish
- Sour cream for garnish (optional)
- Tortilla chips for serving

Instructions:

In a large pot, heat the olive oil over medium heat. Add the chopped onion and cook until softened, about 5 minutes.
Add minced garlic, chopped red bell pepper, and minced jalapeño. Cook for an additional 3-4 minutes until the vegetables are tender.
Stir in ground cumin, chili powder, and smoked paprika. Cook for another minute until fragrant.
Add drained and rinsed black beans, diced tomatoes (with their juices), vegetable or chicken broth, and corn kernels to the pot. Bring the soup to a simmer.
Season the soup with salt and black pepper to taste. Simmer for 15-20 minutes to allow the flavors to meld.
Stir in the lime juice just before serving.
Taste the soup and adjust the seasoning if necessary.
Ladle the Mexican black bean soup into bowls, and garnish with fresh cilantro and avocado slices.

If desired, add a dollop of sour cream on top and serve with tortilla chips on the side.
Serve hot and enjoy this flavorful and hearty Mexican black bean soup!

Roasted Red Pepper Soup

Ingredients:

- 3 large red bell peppers
- 2 tablespoons olive oil
- 1 onion, chopped
- 3 cloves garlic, minced
- 1 carrot, diced
- 1 celery stalk, diced
- 1 can (14 ounces) diced tomatoes
- 4 cups vegetable or chicken broth
- 1 teaspoon smoked paprika
- 1/2 teaspoon dried thyme
- Salt and black pepper to taste
- 1/4 teaspoon red pepper flakes (optional, for added heat)
- 1 cup heavy cream or coconut milk (for a dairy-free option)
- Fresh basil or parsley for garnish

Instructions:

Preheat the oven to broil. Place the red bell peppers on a baking sheet and broil, turning occasionally, until the skin is charred and blistered. Remove from the oven and place the peppers in a bowl, covering with plastic wrap. Let them steam for about 10 minutes.

Peel the charred skin from the roasted red peppers, remove the seeds, and chop the flesh.

In a large pot, heat olive oil over medium heat. Add chopped onion, minced garlic, diced carrot, and diced celery. Cook until the vegetables are softened, about 5-7 minutes.

Add the roasted red peppers, diced tomatoes, vegetable or chicken broth, smoked paprika, dried thyme, salt, black pepper, and red pepper flakes (if using) to the pot. Bring the soup to a simmer.

Simmer the soup for 15-20 minutes to allow the flavors to meld.

Use an immersion blender to puree the soup until smooth. Alternatively, carefully transfer the soup in batches to a blender and blend until smooth. Be cautious with hot liquids.

Return the blended soup to the pot, and stir in the heavy cream or coconut milk.

Taste the soup and adjust the seasoning if needed.
Simmer the soup for an additional 5 minutes to heat through.
Ladle the roasted red pepper soup into bowls, and garnish with fresh basil or parsley.
Serve hot and enjoy this rich and velvety roasted red pepper soup!

Vegetable Curry Soup

Ingredients:

- 2 tablespoons vegetable oil
- 1 onion, chopped
- 3 cloves garlic, minced
- 1 tablespoon ginger, grated
- 2 tablespoons curry powder
- 1 teaspoon ground cumin
- 1 teaspoon ground coriander
- 1/2 teaspoon turmeric
- 1/4 teaspoon cayenne pepper (adjust to taste)
- 1 can (14 ounces) diced tomatoes
- 1 can (14 ounces) coconut milk
- 4 cups vegetable broth
- 2 carrots, diced
- 1 zucchini, diced
- 1 bell pepper, diced
- 1 cup broccoli florets
- 1 cup cauliflower florets
- Salt and black pepper to taste
- 1 cup spinach or kale, chopped
- Juice of 1 lime
- Fresh cilantro for garnish
- Cooked rice or noodles for serving (optional)

Instructions:

In a large pot, heat vegetable oil over medium heat. Add chopped onion and cook until softened, about 5 minutes.

Add minced garlic and grated ginger to the pot. Cook for an additional 1-2 minutes until fragrant.

Stir in curry powder, ground cumin, ground coriander, turmeric, and cayenne pepper. Cook for another minute until the spices are aromatic.

Add diced tomatoes (with their juices), coconut milk, and vegetable broth to the pot. Bring the soup to a simmer.

Add diced carrots, diced zucchini, diced bell pepper, broccoli florets, and cauliflower florets to the pot. Season with salt and black pepper to taste.

Simmer the soup for 15-20 minutes or until the vegetables are tender.

Stir in chopped spinach or kale and lime juice. Cook for an additional 2-3 minutes until the greens are wilted.

Taste the soup and adjust the seasoning if necessary.

Ladle the vegetable curry soup into bowls, and garnish with fresh cilantro.

If desired, serve the soup over cooked rice or noodles.

Serve hot and enjoy this flavorful and nutritious vegetable curry soup!

Italian Wedding Soup

Ingredients:

For the Meatballs:

- 1/2 pound ground beef
- 1/2 pound ground pork
- 1/2 cup breadcrumbs
- 1/4 cup grated Parmesan cheese
- 1/4 cup chopped fresh parsley
- 1 egg
- 2 cloves garlic, minced
- Salt and black pepper to taste

For the Soup:

- 2 tablespoons olive oil
- 1 onion, chopped
- 2 carrots, diced
- 2 celery stalks, diced
- 3 cloves garlic, minced
- 8 cups chicken broth
- 1 teaspoon dried oregano
- 1 teaspoon dried basil
- 1/2 cup small pasta (such as acini di pepe or orzo)
- 4 cups fresh spinach or kale, chopped
- Salt and black pepper to taste
- Grated Parmesan cheese for serving

Instructions:

In a bowl, combine all the meatball ingredients - ground beef, ground pork, breadcrumbs, Parmesan cheese, chopped parsley, egg, minced garlic, salt, and black pepper. Mix well and shape into small meatballs, about 1 inch in diameter.
In a large pot, heat olive oil over medium heat. Add chopped onion, diced carrots, and diced celery. Cook until the vegetables are softened, about 5 minutes.
Add minced garlic and cook for an additional 1-2 minutes until fragrant.
Pour in the chicken broth and bring the soup to a simmer.

Stir in dried oregano and dried basil.
Gently drop the meatballs into the simmering soup. Cook for 10-15 minutes or until the meatballs are cooked through.
Add small pasta to the pot and cook according to the package instructions or until al dente.
Stir in chopped spinach or kale and cook until wilted.
Season the soup with salt and black pepper to taste.
Ladle the Italian Wedding Soup into bowls, and sprinkle with grated Parmesan cheese.
Serve hot and enjoy this comforting and delicious Italian Wedding Soup!

Clam Chowder

Ingredients:

- 4 slices bacon, chopped
- 1 onion, finely chopped
- 2 celery stalks, finely chopped
- 3 cloves garlic, minced
- 3 tablespoons all-purpose flour
- 4 cups clam juice (from canned clams)
- 4 cups potatoes, peeled and diced
- 2 cups half-and-half
- 2 bay leaves
- 1 teaspoon dried thyme
- Salt and black pepper to taste
- 2 cans (6.5 ounces each) chopped clams, drained (reserve the juice)
- Fresh parsley for garnish
- Oyster crackers for serving

Instructions:

In a large pot, cook the chopped bacon over medium heat until crispy. Remove the bacon and set it aside, leaving the bacon fat in the pot.
Add chopped onion, chopped celery, and minced garlic to the pot. Cook until the vegetables are softened, about 5 minutes.
Sprinkle flour over the vegetables and stir to combine. Cook for an additional 2 minutes to eliminate the raw flour taste.
Slowly whisk in the clam juice, ensuring there are no lumps. Add diced potatoes, half-and-half, bay leaves, dried thyme, salt, and black pepper to the pot.
Bring the chowder to a simmer and let it cook for 15-20 minutes or until the potatoes are tender.
Stir in the drained chopped clams and the reserved clam juice. Cook for an additional 5 minutes.
Taste the chowder and adjust the seasoning if necessary.
Remove the bay leaves from the pot.
Ladle the clam chowder into bowls, and garnish with the reserved crispy bacon, fresh parsley, and oyster crackers.
Serve hot and enjoy this classic New England Clam Chowder!

Chicken and Rice Soup

Ingredients:

- 1 tablespoon olive oil
- 1 onion, chopped
- 3 carrots, diced
- 3 celery stalks, diced
- 3 cloves garlic, minced
- 1 pound (about 2 cups) boneless, skinless chicken breasts, diced
- 1 cup white rice, uncooked
- 8 cups chicken broth
- 1 teaspoon dried thyme
- 1 bay leaf
- Salt and black pepper to taste
- Fresh parsley for garnish (optional)
- Lemon wedges for serving (optional)

Instructions:

In a large pot, heat the olive oil over medium heat. Add the chopped onion, diced carrots, and diced celery. Cook until the vegetables are softened, about 5-7 minutes.
Add minced garlic and cook for an additional 1-2 minutes until fragrant.
Add diced chicken to the pot and cook until the chicken is no longer pink.
Stir in uncooked white rice, chicken broth, dried thyme, bay leaf, salt, and black pepper.
Bring the soup to a boil, then reduce the heat to low, cover, and simmer for 15-20 minutes or until the rice is cooked and the chicken is tender.
Remove the bay leaf from the pot.
Taste the soup and adjust the seasoning if necessary.
Ladle the chicken and rice soup into bowls, and garnish with fresh parsley if desired.
Serve hot, and if desired, squeeze a bit of fresh lemon juice into each bowl for a burst of flavor.
Enjoy this hearty and comforting chicken and rice soup!

Sweet Potato and Kale Soup

Ingredients:

- 2 tablespoons olive oil
- 1 onion, chopped
- 3 cloves garlic, minced
- 2 sweet potatoes, peeled and diced
- 1 teaspoon ground cumin
- 1/2 teaspoon ground coriander
- 1/2 teaspoon smoked paprika
- 6 cups vegetable broth
- 1 bunch kale, stems removed and leaves chopped
- Salt and black pepper to taste
- 1 can (14 ounces) white beans, drained and rinsed
- Juice of 1 lemon
- Greek yogurt or sour cream for serving (optional)

Instructions:

In a large pot, heat the olive oil over medium heat. Add the chopped onion and cook until softened, about 5 minutes.
Add minced garlic and cook for an additional 1-2 minutes until fragrant.
Stir in diced sweet potatoes, ground cumin, ground coriander, and smoked paprika. Cook for another 5 minutes.
Pour in the vegetable broth and bring the soup to a simmer. Cook for 15-20 minutes or until the sweet potatoes are tender.
Add chopped kale to the pot and cook until wilted, about 3-5 minutes.
Season the soup with salt and black pepper to taste.
Stir in white beans and let them heat through.
Squeeze in the juice of 1 lemon and stir to combine.
Taste the soup and adjust the seasoning if necessary.
Ladle the sweet potato and kale soup into bowls, and if desired, add a dollop of Greek yogurt or sour cream on top.
Serve hot and enjoy this nutritious and flavorful sweet potato and kale soup!

Moroccan Chickpea Soup

Ingredients:

- 2 tablespoons olive oil
- 1 onion, finely chopped
- 3 cloves garlic, minced
- 1 carrot, diced
- 1 celery stalk, diced
- 1 teaspoon ground cumin
- 1 teaspoon ground coriander
- 1/2 teaspoon ground turmeric
- 1/2 teaspoon ground cinnamon
- 1/4 teaspoon cayenne pepper (adjust to taste)
- 1 can (14 ounces) diced tomatoes
- 1 can (15 ounces) chickpeas, drained and rinsed
- 4 cups vegetable broth
- 1/2 cup red lentils
- 1 sweet potato, peeled and diced
- Salt and black pepper to taste
- Juice of 1 lemon
- Fresh cilantro or parsley for garnish
- Greek yogurt for serving (optional)

Instructions:

In a large pot, heat the olive oil over medium heat. Add the chopped onion, diced carrot, and diced celery. Cook until the vegetables are softened, about 5-7 minutes.
Add minced garlic and cook for an additional 1-2 minutes until fragrant.
Stir in ground cumin, ground coriander, ground turmeric, ground cinnamon, and cayenne pepper. Cook for another minute until the spices are aromatic.
Add diced tomatoes, chickpeas, vegetable broth, red lentils, and diced sweet potato to the pot. Season with salt and black pepper to taste.
Bring the soup to a simmer and let it cook for 20-25 minutes or until the lentils and sweet potato are tender.
Stir in the lemon juice just before serving.
Taste the soup and adjust the seasoning if necessary.

Ladle the Moroccan chickpea soup into bowls, and garnish with fresh cilantro or parsley.
If desired, serve the soup with a dollop of Greek yogurt on top.
Serve hot and enjoy this aromatic and flavorful Moroccan chickpea soup!

Lemon Chicken Orzo Soup

Ingredients:

- 1 tablespoon olive oil
- 1 onion, chopped
- 2 carrots, diced
- 2 celery stalks, diced
- 3 cloves garlic, minced
- 1 pound boneless, skinless chicken breasts, diced
- 8 cups chicken broth
- 1 cup orzo pasta
- 1 teaspoon dried thyme
- 1 bay leaf
- Salt and black pepper to taste
- Juice of 2 lemons
- Zest of 1 lemon
- 2 cups baby spinach or kale, chopped
- Fresh parsley for garnish (optional)

Instructions:

In a large pot, heat olive oil over medium heat. Add chopped onion, diced carrots, and diced celery. Cook until the vegetables are softened, about 5-7 minutes.
Add minced garlic and cook for an additional 1-2 minutes until fragrant.
Add diced chicken to the pot and cook until the chicken is no longer pink.
Pour in the chicken broth, and add orzo pasta, dried thyme, bay leaf, salt, and black pepper.
Bring the soup to a boil, then reduce the heat to low, cover, and simmer for 10-12 minutes or until the orzo is cooked.
Remove the bay leaf from the pot.
Stir in the lemon juice and lemon zest.
Add chopped baby spinach or kale to the pot and cook until wilted.
Taste the soup and adjust the seasoning if necessary.
Ladle the lemon chicken orzo soup into bowls, and garnish with fresh parsley if desired.
Serve hot and enjoy this bright and comforting soup with a hint of lemon flavor!

Creamy Cauliflower Soup

Ingredients:

- 2 tablespoons butter or olive oil
- 1 onion, chopped
- 3 cloves garlic, minced
- 1 head cauliflower, chopped into florets
- 4 cups vegetable or chicken broth
- 1 medium potato, peeled and diced
- 1 teaspoon dried thyme
- Salt and black pepper to taste
- 2 cups milk or vegetable broth
- 1/2 cup heavy cream (optional)
- Grated Parmesan cheese for garnish (optional)
- Fresh chives or parsley for garnish

Instructions:

In a large pot, melt the butter or heat the olive oil over medium heat. Add the chopped onion and cook until softened, about 5 minutes.
Add minced garlic and cook for an additional 1-2 minutes until fragrant.
Add chopped cauliflower florets, diced potato, vegetable or chicken broth, dried thyme, salt, and black pepper to the pot. Bring the soup to a simmer.
Cover the pot and let it cook for 20-25 minutes or until the cauliflower and potatoes are tender.
Use an immersion blender to puree the soup until smooth. Alternatively, transfer the soup in batches to a blender and blend until smooth. Be cautious with hot liquids.
Return the blended soup to the pot and stir in milk or vegetable broth.
If using, add heavy cream for extra creaminess. Stir well.
Taste the soup and adjust the seasoning if necessary.
Simmer the soup for an additional 5-10 minutes to heat through.
Ladle the creamy cauliflower soup into bowls, and garnish with grated Parmesan cheese, fresh chives, or parsley.
Serve hot and enjoy this velvety and nutritious creamy cauliflower soup!

Shrimp and Corn Chowder

Ingredients:

- 2 tablespoons butter
- 1 onion, finely chopped
- 2 cloves garlic, minced
- 2 carrots, diced
- 2 celery stalks, diced
- 1 red bell pepper, diced
- 1/4 cup all-purpose flour
- 4 cups chicken broth
- 2 cups milk
- 1 teaspoon dried thyme
- 1 bay leaf
- 4 cups corn kernels (fresh or frozen)
- 1 pound shrimp, peeled and deveined
- Salt and black pepper to taste
- 1/2 cup heavy cream
- Fresh parsley for garnish

Instructions:

In a large pot, melt the butter over medium heat. Add chopped onion, minced garlic, diced carrots, diced celery, and diced red bell pepper. Cook until the vegetables are softened, about 5-7 minutes.
Sprinkle flour over the vegetables and stir to combine. Cook for an additional 2-3 minutes to eliminate the raw flour taste.
Gradually whisk in chicken broth, ensuring there are no lumps. Add milk, dried thyme, and the bay leaf. Bring the mixture to a simmer.
Stir in corn kernels and let the chowder simmer for 10-15 minutes, allowing the flavors to meld and the corn to cook.
Add shrimp to the pot and cook until they turn pink and opaque, about 3-5 minutes.
Season the chowder with salt and black pepper to taste.
Remove the bay leaf from the pot.
Stir in heavy cream and let the chowder simmer for an additional 2-3 minutes.
Taste the chowder and adjust the seasoning if necessary.

Ladle the shrimp and corn chowder into bowls, and garnish with fresh parsley. Serve hot and enjoy this rich and flavorful shrimp and corn chowder!

Spinach and White Bean Soup

Ingredients:

- 2 tablespoons olive oil
- 1 onion, chopped
- 3 cloves garlic, minced
- 2 carrots, diced
- 2 celery stalks, diced
- 1 teaspoon dried thyme
- 2 cans (15 ounces each) white beans, drained and rinsed
- 6 cups vegetable or chicken broth
- 1 can (14 ounces) diced tomatoes
- 1 teaspoon dried rosemary
- Salt and black pepper to taste
- 4 cups fresh spinach, chopped
- Juice of 1 lemon
- Grated Parmesan cheese for serving (optional)

Instructions:

In a large pot, heat olive oil over medium heat. Add chopped onion, minced garlic, diced carrots, and diced celery. Cook until the vegetables are softened, about 5-7 minutes.
Stir in dried thyme and cook for an additional minute.
Add drained and rinsed white beans, vegetable or chicken broth, diced tomatoes (with their juices), dried rosemary, salt, and black pepper to the pot. Bring the soup to a simmer.
Simmer the soup for 15-20 minutes to allow the flavors to meld.
Add chopped fresh spinach to the pot and cook until wilted.
Squeeze in the juice of 1 lemon and stir to combine.
Taste the soup and adjust the seasoning if necessary.
Ladle the spinach and white bean soup into bowls, and if desired, sprinkle with grated Parmesan cheese.
Serve hot and enjoy this hearty and nutritious spinach and white bean soup!

Turkey Chili

Ingredients:

- 1 tablespoon olive oil
- 1 onion, chopped
- 3 cloves garlic, minced
- 1 pound ground turkey
- 1 bell pepper, chopped
- 1 jalapeño, seeded and minced
- 2 cans (15 ounces each) black beans, drained and rinsed
- 1 can (15 ounces) kidney beans, drained and rinsed
- 1 can (14 ounces) diced tomatoes
- 1 can (6 ounces) tomato paste
- 2 cups chicken broth
- 2 teaspoons chili powder
- 1 teaspoon ground cumin
- 1 teaspoon dried oregano
- 1/2 teaspoon smoked paprika
- Salt and black pepper to taste
- Optional toppings: shredded cheese, chopped green onions, sour cream, cilantro, avocado

Instructions:

In a large pot, heat olive oil over medium heat. Add chopped onion and minced garlic. Cook until the onion is softened, about 5 minutes.

Add ground turkey to the pot and cook until browned, breaking it up with a spoon as it cooks.

Stir in chopped bell pepper and minced jalapeño. Cook for an additional 3-4 minutes.

Add black beans, kidney beans, diced tomatoes, tomato paste, and chicken broth to the pot. Stir to combine.

Season the chili with chili powder, ground cumin, dried oregano, smoked paprika, salt, and black pepper.

Bring the chili to a simmer, then reduce the heat to low and let it simmer for at least 30 minutes to allow the flavors to meld.

Taste the chili and adjust the seasoning if necessary.

Serve the turkey chili hot, and top with shredded cheese, chopped green onions, sour cream, cilantro, and avocado if desired.
Enjoy this delicious and hearty turkey chili!

Broccoli Cheddar Soup

Ingredients:

- 4 tablespoons unsalted butter
- 1 onion, chopped
- 3 cloves garlic, minced
- 1/4 cup all-purpose flour
- 4 cups vegetable or chicken broth
- 4 cups broccoli florets
- 2 carrots, grated
- 2 cups milk
- 2 cups shredded sharp cheddar cheese
- Salt and black pepper to taste
- 1/2 teaspoon nutmeg (optional, for added flavor)
- Dash of cayenne pepper (optional, for a hint of heat)
- Croutons or additional shredded cheese for garnish (optional)

Instructions:

In a large pot, melt the butter over medium heat. Add chopped onion and cook until softened, about 5 minutes.

Add minced garlic and cook for an additional 1-2 minutes until fragrant.

Sprinkle flour over the onion and garlic, stirring constantly to create a roux. Cook for 2-3 minutes to eliminate the raw flour taste.

Gradually whisk in the vegetable or chicken broth, ensuring there are no lumps.

Add broccoli florets and grated carrots to the pot. Simmer for 15-20 minutes or until the vegetables are tender.

Using an immersion blender, blend the soup until it reaches your desired level of smoothness. Alternatively, transfer the soup in batches to a blender and blend until smooth. Be cautious with hot liquids.

Return the blended soup to the pot and stir in milk.

Gradually add shredded cheddar cheese to the pot, stirring continuously until the cheese is melted and the soup is smooth.

Season the soup with salt, black pepper, nutmeg (if using), and cayenne pepper (if using).

Taste the soup and adjust the seasoning if necessary.

Ladle the broccoli cheddar soup into bowls, and if desired, garnish with croutons or additional shredded cheese.
Serve hot and enjoy this rich and comforting broccoli cheddar soup!

Sausage and Kale Soup

Ingredients:

- 1 tablespoon olive oil
- 1 pound Italian sausage, casings removed
- 1 onion, chopped
- 3 cloves garlic, minced
- 2 carrots, diced
- 2 celery stalks, diced
- 1 teaspoon dried thyme
- 1 teaspoon dried rosemary
- 1 bay leaf
- 6 cups chicken broth
- 4 cups chopped kale, stems removed
- Salt and black pepper to taste
- 1 can (14 ounces) diced tomatoes
- 1 can (14 ounces) white beans, drained and rinsed
- Grated Parmesan cheese for garnish (optional)

Instructions:

In a large pot, heat the olive oil over medium heat. Add the Italian sausage, breaking it up with a spoon, and cook until browned.
Add chopped onion, minced garlic, diced carrots, and diced celery to the pot. Cook until the vegetables are softened, about 5-7 minutes.
Stir in dried thyme, dried rosemary, and the bay leaf. Cook for an additional minute.
Pour in the chicken broth and bring the soup to a simmer.
Add chopped kale to the pot and simmer for 10-15 minutes or until the kale is tender.
Season the soup with salt and black pepper to taste.
Stir in diced tomatoes (with their juices) and drained white beans. Simmer for an additional 5-7 minutes.
Remove the bay leaf from the pot.
Taste the soup and adjust the seasoning if necessary.
Ladle the sausage and kale soup into bowls, and if desired, garnish with grated Parmesan cheese.

Serve hot and enjoy this hearty and flavorful sausage and kale soup!

Zucchini and Corn Chowder

Ingredients:

- 2 tablespoons butter
- 1 onion, chopped
- 2 cloves garlic, minced
- 3 zucchini, diced
- 2 potatoes, peeled and diced
- 4 cups vegetable or chicken broth
- 2 cups corn kernels (fresh or frozen)
- 1 teaspoon dried thyme
- 1 bay leaf
- Salt and black pepper to taste
- 2 cups milk
- 1/2 cup heavy cream (optional)
- Fresh parsley for garnish
- Grated Parmesan cheese for serving (optional)

Instructions:

In a large pot, melt the butter over medium heat. Add chopped onion and cook until softened, about 5 minutes.
Add minced garlic and cook for an additional 1-2 minutes until fragrant.
Add diced zucchini and potatoes to the pot. Cook for 5-7 minutes until the vegetables start to soften.
Pour in the vegetable or chicken broth and bring the soup to a simmer.
Add corn kernels, dried thyme, bay leaf, salt, and black pepper to the pot. Simmer for 15-20 minutes or until the vegetables are tender.
Remove the bay leaf from the pot.
Stir in milk and, if using, add heavy cream for extra creaminess.
Taste the chowder and adjust the seasoning if necessary.
Simmer the soup for an additional 5 minutes to heat through.
Ladle the zucchini and corn chowder into bowls, and garnish with fresh parsley.
If desired, sprinkle with grated Parmesan cheese before serving.
Serve hot and enjoy this light and delicious zucchini and corn chowder!

Carrot Ginger Soup

Ingredients:

- 2 tablespoons olive oil
- 1 onion, chopped
- 2 pounds carrots, peeled and chopped
- 3 cloves garlic, minced
- 1 tablespoon fresh ginger, grated
- 4 cups vegetable or chicken broth
- 1 teaspoon ground cumin
- 1/2 teaspoon ground coriander
- Salt and black pepper to taste
- 1 can (14 ounces) coconut milk
- Juice of 1 orange
- Fresh cilantro for garnish
- Toasted pumpkin seeds for garnish (optional)

Instructions:

In a large pot, heat the olive oil over medium heat. Add chopped onion and cook until softened, about 5 minutes.

Add chopped carrots, minced garlic, and grated ginger to the pot. Cook for an additional 5-7 minutes until the carrots start to soften.

Pour in the vegetable or chicken broth, ground cumin, ground coriander, salt, and black pepper. Bring the soup to a simmer and cook for 15-20 minutes or until the carrots are tender.

Use an immersion blender to puree the soup until smooth. Alternatively, transfer the soup in batches to a blender and blend until smooth. Be cautious with hot liquids.

Return the blended soup to the pot and stir in coconut milk.

Squeeze in the juice of 1 orange and stir to combine.

Taste the soup and adjust the seasoning if necessary.

Simmer the soup for an additional 5 minutes to heat through.

Ladle the carrot ginger soup into bowls, and garnish with fresh cilantro and toasted pumpkin seeds if desired.

Serve hot and enjoy this vibrant and flavorful carrot ginger soup!

Quinoa and Vegetable Soup

Ingredients:

- 1 cup quinoa, rinsed
- 2 tablespoons olive oil
- 1 onion, chopped
- 3 cloves garlic, minced
- 2 carrots, diced
- 2 celery stalks, diced
- 1 bell pepper, diced
- 1 zucchini, diced
- 1 can (14 ounces) diced tomatoes
- 8 cups vegetable broth
- 1 teaspoon dried thyme
- 1 teaspoon ground cumin
- 1 teaspoon smoked paprika
- Salt and black pepper to taste
- 2 cups spinach or kale, chopped
- Juice of 1 lemon
- Fresh parsley for garnish

Instructions:

In a fine-mesh sieve, rinse quinoa under cold water.
In a large pot, heat olive oil over medium heat. Add chopped onion and cook until softened, about 5 minutes.
Add minced garlic, diced carrots, diced celery, diced bell pepper, and diced zucchini to the pot. Cook for an additional 5-7 minutes until the vegetables start to soften.
Stir in rinsed quinoa, diced tomatoes (with their juices), vegetable broth, dried thyme, ground cumin, smoked paprika, salt, and black pepper. Bring the soup to a simmer.
Simmer the soup for 15-20 minutes or until the quinoa and vegetables are cooked.
Add chopped spinach or kale to the pot and cook until wilted.
Squeeze in the juice of 1 lemon and stir to combine.
Taste the soup and adjust the seasoning if necessary.

Ladle the quinoa and vegetable soup into bowls, and garnish with fresh parsley. Serve hot and enjoy this wholesome and nutritious quinoa and vegetable soup!

Creamy Chicken and Wild Rice Soup

Ingredients:

- 1 cup wild rice, uncooked
- 4 cups chicken broth
- 1 pound boneless, skinless chicken breasts, diced
- 3 tablespoons butter
- 1 onion, chopped
- 2 carrots, diced
- 2 celery stalks, diced
- 3 cloves garlic, minced
- 1/2 cup all-purpose flour
- 4 cups milk
- 1 cup heavy cream
- 1 teaspoon dried thyme
- 1 bay leaf
- Salt and black pepper to taste
- Fresh parsley for garnish

Instructions:

In a medium saucepan, combine wild rice and chicken broth. Bring to a boil, then reduce the heat to low, cover, and simmer for 45-50 minutes or until the rice is cooked and tender.

In a large pot, cook diced chicken in a bit of oil until browned. Remove chicken from the pot and set aside.

In the same pot, melt butter over medium heat. Add chopped onion, diced carrots, diced celery, and minced garlic. Cook until the vegetables are softened, about 5-7 minutes.

Sprinkle flour over the vegetables and stir to combine. Cook for an additional 2-3 minutes to eliminate the raw flour taste.

Gradually whisk in milk and heavy cream, ensuring there are no lumps.

Add cooked wild rice, diced chicken, dried thyme, bay leaf, salt, and black pepper to the pot. Bring the soup to a simmer.

Simmer the soup for 15-20 minutes to allow the flavors to meld and the soup to thicken.

Remove the bay leaf from the pot.

Taste the soup and adjust the seasoning if necessary.
Ladle the creamy chicken and wild rice soup into bowls, and garnish with fresh parsley.
Serve hot and enjoy this rich and comforting soup!

Black-eyed Pea Soup

Ingredients:

- 1 cup dried black-eyed peas, soaked overnight and drained
- 2 tablespoons olive oil
- 1 onion, chopped
- 2 carrots, diced
- 2 celery stalks, diced
- 3 cloves garlic, minced
- 1 bell pepper, diced
- 1 can (14 ounces) diced tomatoes
- 6 cups vegetable or chicken broth
- 1 teaspoon dried thyme
- 1 bay leaf
- 1 teaspoon smoked paprika
- 1/2 teaspoon cayenne pepper (adjust to taste)
- Salt and black pepper to taste
- 2 cups chopped collard greens or spinach
- Juice of 1 lemon
- Fresh parsley for garnish

Instructions:

In a large pot, heat olive oil over medium heat. Add chopped onion, diced carrots, diced celery, minced garlic, and diced bell pepper. Cook until the vegetables are softened, about 5-7 minutes.
Add soaked and drained black-eyed peas to the pot.
Stir in diced tomatoes (with their juices), vegetable or chicken broth, dried thyme, bay leaf, smoked paprika, cayenne pepper, salt, and black pepper. Bring the soup to a simmer.
Simmer the soup for 45-60 minutes or until the black-eyed peas are tender.
Add chopped collard greens or spinach to the pot and cook until wilted.
Squeeze in the juice of 1 lemon and stir to combine.
Taste the soup and adjust the seasoning if necessary.
Remove the bay leaf from the pot.
Ladle the black-eyed pea soup into bowls, and garnish with fresh parsley.
Serve hot and enjoy this hearty and flavorful black-eyed pea soup!

Cabbage Roll Soup

Ingredients:

- 1 pound ground beef
- 1 onion, chopped
- 2 cloves garlic, minced
- 1 cup rice, uncooked
- 1 head cabbage, chopped
- 1 can (14 ounces) diced tomatoes
- 1 can (8 ounces) tomato sauce
- 6 cups beef broth
- 1 teaspoon dried thyme
- 1 teaspoon paprika
- Salt and black pepper to taste
- 1 bay leaf
- Fresh parsley for garnish
- Sour cream for serving (optional)

Instructions:

In a large pot, brown the ground beef over medium heat, breaking it up with a spoon as it cooks.
Add chopped onion and minced garlic to the pot. Cook until the onion is softened, about 5 minutes.
Stir in uncooked rice, chopped cabbage, diced tomatoes (with their juices), tomato sauce, beef broth, dried thyme, paprika, salt, black pepper, and the bay leaf.
Bring the soup to a boil, then reduce the heat to low, cover, and simmer for 25-30 minutes or until the rice and cabbage are tender.
Taste the soup and adjust the seasoning if necessary.
Remove the bay leaf from the pot.
Ladle the cabbage roll soup into bowls, and garnish with fresh parsley.
If desired, serve the soup with a dollop of sour cream on top.
Serve hot and enjoy this deconstructed and flavorful cabbage roll soup!

Hungarian Goulash Soup

Ingredients:

- 2 tablespoons vegetable oil
- 1 onion, finely chopped
- 2 cloves garlic, minced
- 1 1/2 pounds beef stew meat, cut into bite-sized cubes
- 2 tablespoons sweet paprika
- 1 teaspoon caraway seeds
- 1 teaspoon dried thyme
- 2 tablespoons tomato paste
- 1 tablespoon flour
- 1 red bell pepper, diced
- 1 yellow bell pepper, diced
- 2 carrots, sliced
- 2 potatoes, peeled and diced
- 6 cups beef broth
- 1 bay leaf
- Salt and black pepper to taste
- Chopped fresh parsley for garnish
- Sour cream for serving (optional)

Instructions:

In a large pot, heat vegetable oil over medium heat. Add chopped onion and cook until softened, about 5 minutes.

Add minced garlic and cook for an additional 1-2 minutes until fragrant.

Add beef stew meat to the pot and cook until browned on all sides.

Stir in sweet paprika, caraway seeds, dried thyme, tomato paste, and flour. Cook for 2-3 minutes to enhance the flavors.

Add diced red and yellow bell peppers, sliced carrots, and diced potatoes to the pot.

Pour in beef broth and add the bay leaf. Bring the soup to a simmer.

Season the goulash soup with salt and black pepper to taste.

Simmer the soup for 1.5 to 2 hours or until the beef is tender and the flavors have melded.

Remove the bay leaf from the pot.

Taste the soup and adjust the seasoning if necessary.
Ladle the Hungarian goulash soup into bowls, and garnish with chopped fresh parsley.
If desired, serve with a dollop of sour cream on top.
Serve hot and enjoy this hearty and flavorful Hungarian goulash soup!

Mediterranean Fish Soup

Ingredients:

- 2 tablespoons olive oil
- 1 onion, finely chopped
- 2 cloves garlic, minced
- 1 fennel bulb, thinly sliced
- 1 red bell pepper, diced
- 1 yellow bell pepper, diced
- 1 teaspoon dried oregano
- 1 teaspoon dried thyme
- 1 teaspoon smoked paprika
- 1/2 teaspoon crushed red pepper flakes (adjust to taste)
- 1 can (14 ounces) diced tomatoes
- 4 cups fish or vegetable broth
- 1 cup dry white wine
- 1 pound white fish fillets, cut into bite-sized pieces
- 1/2 pound shrimp, peeled and deveined
- Salt and black pepper to taste
- Juice of 1 lemon
- Fresh parsley for garnish
- Crusty bread for serving

Instructions:

In a large pot, heat olive oil over medium heat. Add chopped onion and cook until softened, about 5 minutes.
Add minced garlic, sliced fennel, diced red and yellow bell peppers, dried oregano, dried thyme, smoked paprika, and crushed red pepper flakes. Cook for an additional 5-7 minutes until the vegetables are softened.
Stir in diced tomatoes (with their juices), fish or vegetable broth, and white wine. Bring the soup to a simmer.
Add white fish fillets and shrimp to the pot. Cook for 5-7 minutes or until the fish is opaque and the shrimp are pink and cooked through.
Season the soup with salt and black pepper to taste.
Squeeze in the juice of 1 lemon and stir to combine.
Taste the soup and adjust the seasoning if necessary.

Ladle the Mediterranean fish soup into bowls, and garnish with fresh parsley.
Serve hot with crusty bread on the side.
Enjoy this delightful and flavorful Mediterranean fish soup!

Pumpkin Curry Soup

Ingredients:

- 2 tablespoons olive oil
- 1 onion, chopped
- 3 cloves garlic, minced
- 1 tablespoon fresh ginger, grated
- 2 tablespoons red curry paste
- 1 can (15 ounces) pumpkin puree
- 4 cups vegetable or chicken broth
- 1 can (14 ounces) coconut milk
- 1 teaspoon ground turmeric
- 1 teaspoon ground cumin
- 1/2 teaspoon ground coriander
- Salt and black pepper to taste
- 1 tablespoon soy sauce
- 1 tablespoon maple syrup or honey
- Juice of 1 lime
- Fresh cilantro for garnish
- Toasted pumpkin seeds for garnish (optional)

Instructions:

In a large pot, heat olive oil over medium heat. Add chopped onion and cook until softened, about 5 minutes.
Add minced garlic and grated ginger to the pot. Cook for an additional 1-2 minutes until fragrant.
Stir in red curry paste and cook for 1-2 minutes to enhance the flavors.
Add pumpkin puree, vegetable or chicken broth, and coconut milk to the pot. Whisk until smooth.
Stir in ground turmeric, ground cumin, ground coriander, salt, and black pepper.
Bring the soup to a simmer and let it cook for 15-20 minutes to allow the flavors to meld.
Add soy sauce, maple syrup or honey, and lime juice to the pot. Stir to combine.
Taste the soup and adjust the seasoning if necessary.
Ladle the pumpkin curry soup into bowls, and garnish with fresh cilantro and toasted pumpkin seeds if desired.

Serve hot and enjoy this comforting and aromatic pumpkin curry soup!

Lemon Dill Chicken Soup

Ingredients:

- 1 tablespoon olive oil
- 1 onion, chopped
- 2 carrots, diced
- 2 celery stalks, diced
- 3 cloves garlic, minced
- 1 pound boneless, skinless chicken breasts, diced
- 8 cups chicken broth
- 1/2 cup orzo pasta
- 1 teaspoon dried dill
- Salt and black pepper to taste
- Juice of 2 lemons
- Zest of 1 lemon
- 1/2 cup chopped fresh dill
- Fresh parsley for garnish (optional)

Instructions:

In a large pot, heat olive oil over medium heat. Add chopped onion, diced carrots, and diced celery. Cook until the vegetables are softened, about 5-7 minutes.
Add minced garlic and cook for an additional 1-2 minutes until fragrant.
Add diced chicken to the pot and cook until browned.
Pour in the chicken broth and bring the soup to a simmer.
Add orzo pasta, dried dill, salt, and black pepper to the pot. Simmer for 10-12 minutes or until the orzo is cooked.
Stir in the juice of 2 lemons and the zest of 1 lemon.
Add chopped fresh dill to the pot and stir to combine.
Taste the soup and adjust the seasoning if necessary.
Ladle the lemon dill chicken soup into bowls, and if desired, garnish with fresh parsley.
Serve hot and enjoy this refreshing and flavorful lemon dill chicken soup!

Thai Tom Yum Soup

Ingredients:

- 4 cups chicken or vegetable broth
- 1 stalk lemongrass, bruised and chopped into 2-inch pieces
- 3 kaffir lime leaves, torn into pieces
- 3-4 slices galangal or ginger
- 2 Thai bird's eye chilies, smashed (adjust to taste)
- 200g (7 oz) shrimp, peeled and deveined
- 200g (7 oz) mushrooms, sliced
- 1 medium tomato, cut into wedges
- 1 small onion, sliced
- 2 tablespoons fish sauce
- 1 tablespoon soy sauce
- 1 teaspoon sugar
- Juice of 2 limes
- Fresh cilantro leaves for garnish
- Thai bird's eye chilies for extra spice (optional)

Instructions:

In a pot, bring the chicken or vegetable broth to a simmer.
Add lemongrass, kaffir lime leaves, galangal or ginger, and smashed Thai bird's eye chilies. Simmer for 5-10 minutes to infuse the broth with flavors.
Add shrimp, mushrooms, tomato wedges, and sliced onion to the pot. Cook until the shrimp turns pink and opaque.
Season the soup with fish sauce, soy sauce, sugar, and lime juice. Adjust the seasoning to your taste.
Discard lemongrass, kaffir lime leaves, and galangal or ginger slices.
Ladle the Tom Yum soup into bowls, and garnish with fresh cilantro leaves.
If you like it spicier, you can add extra Thai bird's eye chilies.
Serve hot and enjoy this aromatic and tangy Thai Tom Yum soup!

Corn and Potato Chowder

Ingredients:

- 2 tablespoons butter
- 1 onion, chopped
- 2 celery stalks, diced
- 3 cloves garlic, minced
- 4 cups corn kernels (fresh or frozen)
- 3 cups potatoes, peeled and diced
- 4 cups vegetable or chicken broth
- 1 teaspoon dried thyme
- 1 bay leaf
- 2 cups milk
- 1/2 cup heavy cream
- Salt and black pepper to taste
- Fresh chives for garnish (optional)
- Grated cheddar cheese for serving (optional)

Instructions:

In a large pot, melt the butter over medium heat. Add chopped onion, diced celery, and minced garlic. Cook until the vegetables are softened, about 5-7 minutes.
Add corn kernels and diced potatoes to the pot. Stir to combine.
Pour in the vegetable or chicken broth, add dried thyme, and toss in the bay leaf. Bring the soup to a simmer.
Simmer the soup for 15-20 minutes or until the potatoes are tender.
Remove the bay leaf from the pot.
Use an immersion blender to partially blend the soup, leaving some chunks for texture. Alternatively, transfer a portion of the soup to a blender and blend until smooth, then return it to the pot.
Stir in milk and heavy cream, and season the chowder with salt and black pepper to taste.
Simmer the soup for an additional 5-10 minutes to heat through.
Taste the chowder and adjust the seasoning if necessary.
Ladle the corn and potato chowder into bowls, and if desired, garnish with fresh chives and grated cheddar cheese.
Serve hot and enjoy this creamy and comforting corn and potato chowder!

Chicken and Dumpling Soup

Ingredients:

For the Soup:

- 2 tablespoons butter
- 1 onion, chopped
- 2 carrots, diced
- 2 celery stalks, diced
- 3 cloves garlic, minced
- 1 pound boneless, skinless chicken thighs, diced
- 8 cups chicken broth
- 1 teaspoon dried thyme
- 1 bay leaf
- Salt and black pepper to taste
- 1 cup frozen peas
- 1/2 cup heavy cream

For the Dumplings:

- 2 cups all-purpose flour
- 1 tablespoon baking powder
- 1/2 teaspoon salt
- 1 cup milk
- 1/4 cup chopped fresh parsley

Instructions:

In a large pot, melt butter over medium heat. Add chopped onion, diced carrots, diced celery, and minced garlic. Cook until the vegetables are softened, about 5-7 minutes.
Add diced chicken to the pot and cook until browned.
Pour in the chicken broth, add dried thyme, and toss in the bay leaf. Bring the soup to a simmer.
Simmer the soup for 15-20 minutes or until the chicken is cooked through.
Season the soup with salt and black pepper to taste.
Stir in frozen peas and heavy cream. Simmer for an additional 5 minutes.

While the soup is simmering, prepare the dumplings. In a bowl, whisk together flour, baking powder, and salt. Add milk and chopped parsley, stirring until just combined.

Drop spoonfuls of the dumpling batter into the simmering soup. Cover the pot and let the dumplings cook for 15-20 minutes, or until they are cooked through and no longer doughy in the center.

Remove the bay leaf from the pot.

Taste the soup and adjust the seasoning if necessary.

Ladle the chicken and dumpling soup into bowls and serve hot.

Enjoy this hearty and comforting chicken and dumpling soup!

Soba Noodle Soup

Ingredients:

For the Broth:

- 6 cups vegetable or chicken broth
- 3 tablespoons soy sauce
- 1 tablespoon mirin (Japanese sweet rice wine)
- 1 tablespoon rice vinegar
- 1 tablespoon miso paste
- 1 tablespoon sesame oil
- 2 cloves garlic, minced
- 1 tablespoon fresh ginger, grated
- 1 teaspoon sugar
- Salt and black pepper to taste

For the Soup:

- 8 ounces soba noodles
- 1 cup shiitake mushrooms, sliced
- 1 cup tofu, cubed
- 1 cup baby spinach leaves
- 2 green onions, sliced
- Sesame seeds for garnish
- Nori sheets, cut into thin strips (optional)

Instructions:

In a large pot, combine vegetable or chicken broth, soy sauce, mirin, rice vinegar, miso paste, sesame oil, minced garlic, grated ginger, sugar, salt, and black pepper. Bring the broth to a simmer and let it cook for 10-15 minutes to allow the flavors to meld.
While the broth is simmering, cook the soba noodles according to the package instructions. Drain and rinse the noodles under cold water to stop the cooking process.
Add sliced shiitake mushrooms and cubed tofu to the simmering broth. Cook for an additional 5-7 minutes until the mushrooms are tender and the tofu is heated through.

Stir in baby spinach leaves until wilted.
Taste the broth and adjust the seasoning if necessary.
Divide the cooked soba noodles among serving bowls.
Ladle the hot broth with mushrooms, tofu, and spinach over the soba noodles.
Garnish with sliced green onions, sesame seeds, and nori strips (if using).
Serve the soba noodle soup immediately and enjoy this delicious and comforting dish!

Cuban Black Bean Soup

Ingredients:

- 2 tablespoons olive oil
- 1 onion, finely chopped
- 1 bell pepper, diced
- 2 celery stalks, diced
- 3 cloves garlic, minced
- 2 teaspoons ground cumin
- 1 teaspoon dried oregano
- 1 teaspoon ground coriander
- 1/2 teaspoon smoked paprika
- 2 cans (15 ounces each) black beans, undrained
- 4 cups vegetable or chicken broth
- 1 bay leaf
- Salt and black pepper to taste
- Juice of 1 lime
- 1/4 cup fresh cilantro, chopped
- Sour cream for serving (optional)
- Sliced green onions for garnish (optional)
- Cooked white rice for serving (optional)

Instructions:

In a large pot, heat olive oil over medium heat. Add chopped onion, diced bell pepper, and diced celery. Cook until the vegetables are softened, about 5-7 minutes.

Add minced garlic, ground cumin, dried oregano, ground coriander, and smoked paprika. Cook for an additional 2-3 minutes until the spices are fragrant.

Rinse and drain one can of black beans. Set aside.

In the pot, add the second can of black beans with their liquid, the rinsed black beans, vegetable or chicken broth, and the bay leaf. Stir to combine.

Bring the soup to a simmer and let it cook for 15-20 minutes, allowing the flavors to meld.

Use an immersion blender to partially blend the soup, leaving some whole beans for texture. Alternatively, transfer a portion of the soup to a blender, blend until smooth, and return it to the pot.

Season the soup with salt, black pepper, and lime juice. Stir in chopped cilantro.

Taste the soup and adjust the seasoning if necessary.
Ladle the Cuban black bean soup into bowls. If desired, garnish with a dollop of sour cream, sliced green onions, and serve with cooked white rice on the side. Serve hot and enjoy this flavorful and hearty Cuban black bean soup!

Irish Potato Soup

Ingredients:

- 2 tablespoons butter
- 1 onion, chopped
- 2 leeks, white and light green parts, sliced
- 3 cloves garlic, minced
- 4 large potatoes, peeled and diced
- 6 cups vegetable or chicken broth
- 1 bay leaf
- Salt and black pepper to taste
- 1 cup milk or heavy cream
- Fresh parsley for garnish

Instructions:

In a large pot, melt butter over medium heat. Add chopped onion, sliced leeks, and minced garlic. Cook until the vegetables are softened, about 5-7 minutes.
Add diced potatoes to the pot and cook for an additional 5 minutes, stirring occasionally.
Pour in vegetable or chicken broth and add the bay leaf. Bring the soup to a simmer.
Season the soup with salt and black pepper to taste.
Simmer the soup for 15-20 minutes or until the potatoes are tender.
Remove the bay leaf from the pot.
Use an immersion blender to partially blend the soup, leaving some chunks for texture. Alternatively, transfer a portion of the soup to a blender and blend until smooth, then return it to the pot.
Stir in milk or heavy cream and heat the soup through.
Taste the soup and adjust the seasoning if necessary.
Ladle the Irish potato soup into bowls, and garnish with fresh parsley.
Serve hot and enjoy this creamy and comforting Irish potato soup!

Chicken Gumbo

Ingredients:

- 1/2 cup vegetable oil
- 1/2 cup all-purpose flour
- 1 onion, finely chopped
- 1 bell pepper, diced
- 2 celery stalks, diced
- 3 cloves garlic, minced
- 1 pound boneless, skinless chicken thighs, diced
- 1 pound andouille sausage, sliced
- 4 cups chicken broth
- 1 can (14 ounces) diced tomatoes
- 1 cup okra, sliced (fresh or frozen)
- 1 cup frozen sliced okra
- 1 teaspoon dried thyme
- 1 bay leaf
- 1 teaspoon smoked paprika
- 1 teaspoon Cajun seasoning
- Salt and black pepper to taste
- 1 cup long-grain white rice, cooked
- Chopped green onions for garnish
- Hot sauce for serving (optional)

Instructions:

In a large pot, make a roux by combining vegetable oil and flour over medium heat. Stir continuously until the roux turns a dark brown color, similar to chocolate (be careful not to burn it).

Add chopped onion, diced bell pepper, diced celery, and minced garlic to the pot. Cook until the vegetables are softened, about 5-7 minutes.

Add diced chicken and sliced andouille sausage to the pot. Cook until the chicken is browned.

Pour in chicken broth and diced tomatoes with their juices. Stir to combine.

Add sliced okra, dried thyme, bay leaf, smoked paprika, Cajun seasoning, salt, and black pepper to the pot. Bring the gumbo to a simmer.

Simmer the gumbo for 30-40 minutes, allowing the flavors to meld and the okra to cook.

Remove the bay leaf from the pot.

Taste the gumbo and adjust the seasoning if necessary.

Serve the chicken gumbo over cooked white rice.

Garnish with chopped green onions.

If desired, offer hot sauce on the side for those who like it spicier.

Enjoy this flavorful and hearty chicken gumbo!

White Bean and Escarole Soup

Ingredients:

- 2 tablespoons olive oil
- 1 onion, chopped
- 2 carrots, diced
- 2 celery stalks, diced
- 3 cloves garlic, minced
- 2 cans (15 ounces each) cannellini beans, drained and rinsed
- 1 head escarole, chopped
- 8 cups vegetable or chicken broth
- 1 teaspoon dried thyme
- 1 bay leaf
- Salt and black pepper to taste
- Crushed red pepper flakes (optional, for heat)
- Grated Parmesan cheese for serving
- Crusty bread for serving

Instructions:

In a large pot, heat olive oil over medium heat. Add chopped onion, diced carrots, and diced celery. Cook until the vegetables are softened, about 5-7 minutes.
Add minced garlic and cook for an additional 1-2 minutes until fragrant.
Stir in cannellini beans, chopped escarole, vegetable or chicken broth, dried thyme, and the bay leaf. Bring the soup to a simmer.
Season the soup with salt and black pepper to taste. If you like a bit of heat, add crushed red pepper flakes to your liking.
Simmer the soup for 15-20 minutes or until the escarole is tender.
Remove the bay leaf from the pot.
Taste the soup and adjust the seasoning if necessary.
Ladle the white bean and escarole soup into bowls, and if desired, top with grated Parmesan cheese.
Serve hot with crusty bread on the side.
Enjoy this nutritious and comforting white bean and escarole soup!

Tofu Miso Soup

Ingredients:

- 4 cups vegetable broth
- 3 tablespoons miso paste (white or light miso)
- 1 tablespoon soy sauce
- 1 teaspoon sesame oil
- 1 tablespoon rice vinegar
- 1 teaspoon grated ginger
- 2 green onions, sliced
- 1 cup mushrooms, sliced
- 1 block firm tofu, cubed
- 1 cup spinach leaves
- 2 sheets nori (seaweed), torn into small pieces
- Cooked rice or soba noodles (optional, for serving)

Instructions:

In a pot, bring vegetable broth to a simmer over medium heat.
In a small bowl, mix miso paste with a few tablespoons of hot broth until the miso is fully dissolved. Add this mixture back to the pot.
Stir in soy sauce, sesame oil, rice vinegar, and grated ginger.
Add sliced green onions, mushrooms, cubed tofu, and torn nori sheets to the pot.
Let it simmer for about 5-7 minutes until the mushrooms are cooked and the tofu is heated through.
Stir in spinach leaves until wilted.
Taste the soup and adjust the flavor if necessary, adding more miso paste or soy sauce according to your preference.
If desired, serve the miso soup over cooked rice or soba noodles.
Ladle the tofu miso soup into bowls and enjoy this comforting and flavorful dish!

Tomato and Quinoa Soup

Ingredients:

- 2 tablespoons olive oil
- 1 onion, chopped
- 2 carrots, diced
- 2 celery stalks, diced
- 3 cloves garlic, minced
- 1 can (28 ounces) crushed tomatoes
- 1/2 cup quinoa, rinsed
- 4 cups vegetable broth
- 1 teaspoon dried oregano
- 1 teaspoon dried basil
- 1 bay leaf
- Salt and black pepper to taste
- 1 can (15 ounces) cannellini beans, drained and rinsed
- 2 cups fresh spinach leaves
- 1/4 cup fresh basil, chopped
- Grated Parmesan cheese for serving (optional)

Instructions:

In a large pot, heat olive oil over medium heat. Add chopped onion, diced carrots, and diced celery. Cook until the vegetables are softened, about 5-7 minutes.
Add minced garlic and cook for an additional 1-2 minutes until fragrant.
Stir in crushed tomatoes, rinsed quinoa, vegetable broth, dried oregano, dried basil, and the bay leaf. Bring the soup to a simmer.
Season the soup with salt and black pepper to taste.
Simmer the soup for 15-20 minutes or until the quinoa is cooked.
Add cannellini beans, fresh spinach leaves, and chopped fresh basil to the pot.
Cook until the spinach is wilted.
Remove the bay leaf from the pot.
Taste the soup and adjust the seasoning if necessary.
Ladle the tomato and quinoa soup into bowls, and if desired, top with grated Parmesan cheese.
Serve hot and enjoy this wholesome and satisfying tomato and quinoa soup!

Sweet Corn and Bacon Chowder

Ingredients:

- 6 slices bacon, chopped
- 1 onion, finely chopped
- 2 cloves garlic, minced
- 3 cups sweet corn kernels (fresh or frozen)
- 2 potatoes, peeled and diced
- 4 cups chicken broth
- 1 teaspoon dried thyme
- 1 bay leaf
- Salt and black pepper to taste
- 1 cup whole milk
- 1/2 cup heavy cream
- 1 cup shredded cheddar cheese
- Chopped green onions for garnish
- Crispy bacon bits for garnish

Instructions:

In a large pot, cook the chopped bacon over medium heat until crispy. Remove some for garnish and leave some in the pot.
Add finely chopped onion to the pot and cook until softened, about 5 minutes.
Stir in minced garlic and cook for an additional 1-2 minutes until fragrant.
Add sweet corn kernels and diced potatoes to the pot. Stir to combine.
Pour in chicken broth, add dried thyme, and toss in the bay leaf. Bring the chowder to a simmer.
Season the chowder with salt and black pepper to taste.
Simmer the chowder for 15-20 minutes or until the potatoes are tender.
Remove the bay leaf from the pot.
Stir in whole milk and heavy cream. Let the chowder heat through.
Add shredded cheddar cheese to the pot and stir until melted and combined.
Taste the chowder and adjust the seasoning if necessary.
Ladle the sweet corn and bacon chowder into bowls, and garnish with chopped green onions and crispy bacon bits.
Serve hot and enjoy this creamy and flavorful sweet corn and bacon chowder!

Italian Sausage and Kale Soup

Ingredients:

- 1 tablespoon olive oil
- 1 pound Italian sausage, casings removed
- 1 onion, chopped
- 2 carrots, diced
- 3 cloves garlic, minced
- 1 teaspoon dried oregano
- 1 teaspoon dried basil
- 1/2 teaspoon red pepper flakes (adjust to taste)
- 4 cups chicken broth
- 2 cups water
- 1 can (14 ounces) diced tomatoes
- 1 cup small pasta (such as ditalini or small shells)
- 1 bunch kale, stems removed and leaves chopped
- Salt and black pepper to taste
- Grated Parmesan cheese for serving

Instructions:

In a large pot, heat olive oil over medium heat. Add Italian sausage, breaking it up with a spoon as it cooks, and brown until cooked through.
Add chopped onion and diced carrots to the pot. Cook until the vegetables are softened, about 5-7 minutes.
Stir in minced garlic, dried oregano, dried basil, and red pepper flakes. Cook for an additional 1-2 minutes until fragrant.
Pour in chicken broth, water, and diced tomatoes with their juices. Bring the soup to a simmer.
Add small pasta to the pot and cook according to package instructions until al dente.
Stir in chopped kale and cook until wilted.
Season the soup with salt and black pepper to taste.
Taste the soup and adjust the seasoning if necessary.
Ladle the Italian sausage and kale soup into bowls and serve hot.
Optionally, top each serving with grated Parmesan cheese.
Enjoy this hearty and flavorful Italian sausage and kale soup!

Avocado Lime Chicken Soup

Ingredients:

- 1 tablespoon olive oil
- 1 onion, chopped
- 2 cloves garlic, minced
- 1 pound boneless, skinless chicken breasts, diced
- 6 cups chicken broth
- 1 teaspoon ground cumin
- 1 teaspoon chili powder
- 1/2 teaspoon smoked paprika
- Salt and black pepper to taste
- 1 can (14 ounces) diced tomatoes, undrained
- 1 cup corn kernels (fresh or frozen)
- Juice of 2 limes
- 2 avocados, diced
- Fresh cilantro for garnish
- Tortilla strips or chips for serving

Instructions:

In a large pot, heat olive oil over medium heat. Add chopped onion and cook until softened, about 5 minutes.
Add minced garlic and cook for an additional 1-2 minutes until fragrant.
Add diced chicken to the pot and cook until browned.
Pour in chicken broth, ground cumin, chili powder, smoked paprika, salt, and black pepper. Bring the soup to a simmer.
Stir in diced tomatoes with their juices and corn kernels. Simmer for 10-15 minutes.
Add the juice of 2 limes to the soup.
Just before serving, stir in diced avocados.
Taste the soup and adjust the seasoning if necessary.
Ladle the avocado lime chicken soup into bowls, and garnish with fresh cilantro.
Serve hot with tortilla strips or chips on the side.
Enjoy this refreshing and flavorful avocado lime chicken soup!

www.ingramcontent.com/pod-product-compliance
Lightning Source LLC
LaVergne TN
LVHW081617060526
838201LV00054B/2285